In this series –

RUMI READINGS
FOR
LIFE

RUMI READINGS
FOR
LIFE

JALALUDDIN RUMI

The Scheherazade Foundation

The Scheherazade Foundation CIC
85 Great Portland Street
London
W1W 7LT
United Kingdom
www.SF.Charity
info@SF.Charity

First published by The Scheherazade Foundation CIC, 2025

RUMI READINGS FOR LIFE

© The Scheherazade Foundation

A CIP catalogue record for this title is available from the British Library.

ISBN 978-1-915311-73-3

Introduction

Jalaluddin Rumi was born in Balkh, Afghanistan, in the year 1207, and died in Konya, Turkey, in 1273.

During the sixty-six years spanning this pair of dates, he produced a range of extraordinary work in Persian which, today, is classed as 'Sufi Mysticism'.

In the seven and a half centuries since his death, Rumi's corpus, which includes *The Masnavi* and *Fihi Ma Fihi*, has been circulated widely across the Near East, the Arab world, and Central Asia.

Generations of students continue to commit selections of the 60,000 verses to heart, and allow Rumi's way of thought to permeate through all areas of their lives.

Although Orientalists venturing eastward from Europe in the 1700s occasionally made note of Sufi Mysticism, they tended to witness it through the more theatrical frills – such as 'whirling dervishes' – rather than through a deep appreciation of the texts.

It wasn't until the close of the nineteenth century that the first wholescale translations of Rumi's written work began to appear in Europe.

Even then, they remained very much the purview of a few academics, whose translations were – even for the time – laden with indescribably floral and cumbersome prose.

Although in the Occident, students would find themselves scrutinizing Rumi's corpus, it wasn't until more recently that accessible appreciations of his work became available.

A few years before his death, I asked my father – the Sufi scholar and thinker Idries Shah – for his thoughts on Rumi's legacy in the West.

Sitting in his favourite chair, a porcelain cup of green tea in hand, he looked at me hard.

'I never cease to be amazed,' he said.

'Amazed by what?'

'By the way people don't take what's perfectly packaged, and ready and waiting for them, but rather obsess with something else.'

'With what?'

'With endless and nonsensical trimmings, trappings, and paraphernalia.'

My father sipped his tea.

After a moment of silent thought, he continued:

'Read Rumi in the original Persian,' he said, 'and so delicate are the verses that you have tears rolling down your cheeks. Yet here in the West, it's served up as something submerged in a thick, glutinous gravy, so much so that its utterly inedible.'

I reminded my father that a series of publications had recently found their way to press – publications that presented Rumi's couplets in an utterly new way.

Stripped bare of what my father had referred to as 'gravy', they were light.

Indeed, they were lighter than light.

My father rolled his eyes at the thought.

'In any other place, and at any other time,' he said, 'people would be up in arms. Or, if they weren't, they'd be laughing until their sides split. Imagine it – Western poets with absolutely no knowledge of the original Persian text touting new, bestselling editions of Rumi's work! It's what we call "The Soup of the Soup of the Soup".'

In the years since my father's death, Occidental society has been flooded with all things Rumi.

Couplets ascribed to him are read solemnly at weddings across the United States, Europe, and beyond.

Wisdom drawn from his poetry is tattooed daily over the backs and limbs of Hollywood A-listers.

But the precious words uttered at weddings, tattooed into skin, and quoted in abundance, hold little or no bearing to the original verses of Jalaluddin Rumi.

So, there it is…

The great Sufi Master's wisdom available:

(a) in a form that's unreadable because it's all covered in glutinous gravy, or

(b) in another form that's completely distorted – the Soup of the Soup of the Soup.

One thing that *is* evident is that the West can benefit enormously from a clean, clear rendition of Rumi's thinking – as the East has done over the last seven hundred years.

For this reason, we have commissioned entirely new translations, gleaned in particular from *The Masnavi*. Selected and translated by native Persian-speaking scholars, the emphasis has been on maintaining the lightness of Rumi's poetry.

In an age of relentless speed and digital overload, and so as to allow the work to be accessed by those who may benefit from it most, we have arranged a series of bite-sized morsels by way of theme.

We encourage you to do what students, scholars, and ordinary people have done across the East for centuries…

To pick a single couplet, or a handful – and to read them over and over, allowing them to seed themselves in your mind.

Little by little, having taken root, they will blossom and bear fruit.

Tahir Shah

How to Use This Book

Rumi Readings for Life

This book is about life – not just the idea of it, but the living of it.

The ordinary and the extraordinary. The days that rush by, and the moments that stretch out.

It is about how we walk through time: distracted, curious, uncertain, open.

You do not need to be seeking anything in particular to read this book.

You only need to be alive – and paying attention.

Rumi Readings for Life brings together one hundred quotes drawn from the original Persian works of Jalaluddin Rumi, freshly translated by The Scheherazade Foundation. These are not reinterpretations. They are faithful to the poet's spiritual and psychological insight – rooted in *The Masnavi*, a text designed not for scholars alone, but for everyday people navigating the path of being human.

The quotes are arranged into ten themed sections, each touching on a different aspect of the human experience – from truth and illusion, to sorrow and joy, ethics and effort, fate and freedom. You'll find questions here. Pointers. Mirrors. And reminders of things you may have forgotten in the noise of the world.

This book is not trying to teach you life.
It's here to walk with you while you live it.

A Gentle Invitation

You don't have to read this book from beginning to end.
You don't have to finish it. You don't have to highlight or analyse or make notes.

You are welcome to simply open it – now and then – and let a single line meet you where you are. Let it land. Let it do what it came to do.

Sometimes it may ask something of you.
Sometimes it may simply let you breathe.

You can use it as a kind of calendar – one quote a day, or a week, or as often as you wish. Or you can keep it nearby and open it only when the world becomes a little too much.

There is no right rhythm.

Reflection and Response

Rumi did not write in abstract. His words were always grounded – in body, in breath, in the tangible world. When you read a quote, take a moment. Sit still. Ask yourself:

- What part of me is this speaking to?
- What might I do differently today because of this?
- What does this awaken in my memory – or in my longing?

There is no need to write your answers.

This is not homework. It's an invitation to meet yourself.

Read It Alone or Share It

You may want to read this book in solitude – in the early morning, late at night, or in a pause between things. But you may also find yourself wanting to share a quote with someone – a friend, a partner, a child, a mentor.

Rumi's wisdom, while personal, is also communal. These quotes can offer comfort, shift a conversation, open the space between people.

A single quote can do what an entire speech cannot.

Let It Disrupt You

Some of these quotes may challenge you.

They may disrupt old patterns of thought, familiar beliefs, or assumptions. That's okay. That's part of the work.

Rumi often invites us to flip our perspective – to see what's beneath the surface.

He reminds us that truth can be disorienting before it becomes clarifying.

If something in this book unsettles you, stay with it for a while. Let it ask its question.

All of Life Is Here

This book is called *Rumi Readings for Life* because life is not one thing.

It is not only joy, or sorrow, or seeking. It is all of it.

These pages hold moments of bewilderment and beauty. They hold struggle and surrender. They speak of striving, of patience, of clarity, of rest.

They remind you that you don't need to escape life to touch the divine.

You are already in the middle of it.

Rumi writes in this volume:
'You have nothing but what you strive for; the worth of effort lies in striving for what you want.'

Let this book be part of that effort – not toward perfection, but toward wholeness.

Return to it as you return to yourself.

Again, and again, and again.

Part 1
Life in the Shelter
of Truth

1

He made the world from grace,
and His sun shone on particles of matter.

2

God created us in order to fulfil this purpose: 'We have not created the jinn and mankind except but to worship Me.'

3

Is there a calligrapher
who would write a line beautifully
just for the line's own sake,
without regard to how it reads?
The design appears to be for an unknown reason,
and it is closed for an additional unknown purpose.
Not only for aesthetic appeal and visual exhibition,
but also, for the sake of reading, do calligraphers write.

4

It is confusion,
not this nor that.
The riches must be sought after;
this is destruction.
You lose the true treasure
because of a delusion
that you mistake for a treasure.

5

Transition from existence to absolute nonexistence.
Embrace godliness and seek your Creator.
This worldly existence is merely
a realm of waste;
Beware!
Nonexistence, on the other hand,
is a realm of enrichment.

6

Observe that every rational being
is perpetually in pursuit of nonexistence.
When they plead,
it is for an unattainable benevolence.
In stores, they seek unreal gains.
They are seekers and slaves of nonexistence
who have spurned existence.

7

As life proves profoundly intoxicating,
guilt dissipates from the heart
and reason from the mind.
For millennia, humanity has been led astray
by this intoxication of existence.

8

The steed of nonexistence
is indeed a splendid mount,
for when you are nothing,
it guides you towards genuine existence.
This swift horse of nonexistence
serves as an excellent vehicle,
as it keeps you connected to true life.

9

Within the realms exist both sorrowful,
shadowy souls and pure, radiant spirits.
These entities differ vastly from one another;
while one harbours a precious pearl,
the other possesses a mere semblance of one.
The world was fashioned with the intent of revelation,
ensuring that the hidden treasures of wisdom
remain unearthed.

10

At its core, spiritual existence embodies unity;
division begets duality and polytheism.
Acknowledging the unity of all souls
nurtures a sense of shared destiny
and interconnectedness.

Part 2
The Reflection of Life

11

Creating an escape route
within the confines of the prison
is an act of deception,
and those who seal it are deceitful.
To escape from this world,
likened to a prison
where we are held captive,
one must carve a path
using the chisel of faith.

12

O God,
let not this union dissolve into separation;
let not tears stain the faces of the blissful couple.
Preserve these joyful souls and this garden;
let the garden of the soul flourish and thrive.

13

For such a paltry sum,
what sort of transaction is this –
bartering the soul for a fistful of dust?

14

When the flames of the heart intensify,
both believers and unbelievers are affected;
as the bird of meaning takes flight,
all forms begin to soar.
Suddenly, a tidal wave emerges and crashes
against the verdant dome,
exposing the hidden secret,
and shattering the world's facade.

15

O noble ones,
this world is like a tree,
and we are like its unripe fruits.

16

Its joy is a byproduct
of the fading of pleasure in the world,
be it a drink or a meal.
It was enjoyable and grew pleasurable,
even if it lost its effectiveness due to enjoyment.

17

You enjoy witnessing our conflicts,
which makes us jealous of one another.

18

And that oppressed, lonely soul cries out,
but has no one to listen to it.

19

The city of the eternal
is what the lonely soul on this earth longs for;
why does the animal Self graze here so much?

20

He said,
'These saints are my children,
lonely in a foreign land,
devoid of pomp and circumstance.'
Sometimes you watch from a distance,
because I am a lonely man.

Part 3

Human Beings
& Life Events

21

His presence is evident everywhere you look;
his brightness fills all six directions of the world.

22

There are no intermediaries or means,
Father; all good and evil stem from the Cause.
Except for an illusion
that temporarily veils us
in ignorance along the path.

23

Despite appearing as adversaries and contradictions, day and night intertwine to form a unified reality.

24

Place no reliance on this world;
it is but a fleeting dream.
Whether a hand moves or not matters little
when you are asleep.

25

Beware, for calamity may lurk in your path
if you flee, hoping to find solace elsewhere.
At every turn, there are snares and enemies lying in wait.
True tranquility can only be found
within the shelter of God.

26

Existence, with its intricate illusions,
often presents darkness as light, and light as darkness.
For how else could this world serve
as the very abode of deception?

27

The world, veiled in desire, deceives the senses, leading astray those who succumb to its allure.

28

Let the quill inscribe,
'Every action yields its corresponding consequence.'
If your path is crooked, the script will unveil it;
if virtuous, joy will follow in its wake.

29

O valiant soul,
the Most High subjects us
to heat and cold, suffering and anguish.
Fear, hunger, poverty, and physical ailments:
all laid bare for the scrutiny of the soul.

30

The beaten soldiers opt for defeat,
avoiding confrontation with the underlying problems,
and flee the battlefield in fear for their lives.
But the courageous charge toward the enemy lines,
fighting even as they shake with fear for their lives.

Part 4

The Role of Meaningful Components in Life

31

The path to happiness often winds through valleys of
sorrow, laying the foundation for moments of joy.
Sorrow cleans and clears,
sweeping away the dust of despair from life's abode,
making space for the blossoming joy of compassion.

32

We have a strong affinity
for using precise language and solving puzzles,
almost as if we were in love with these activities.
To complete our personal growth,
we engage in tying and untying knots
in various forms and responses.

33

How fortunate is the one
who experiences a metaphorical death
before their physical death,
for they have already smelled the rose of true
understanding.

34

How many thorns has the hope
of the charming, rose-faced beloved kissed?
How many bearers of burdens
have become moon-like companions
to support their loved one?

35

Act virtuously for the benefit of your Creator,
or for the comfort of your own soul.
Let friendship remain at the forefront of your vision,
and keep hatred and bitterness out of your heart.

36

O son, break free from all ties.
Why be constrained by gold and silver?
How much water can a jug hold if you fill it to the brim?
The pearl is nowhere to be found,
and the jug of the greedy never fills.

37

When, in loneliness, you give up on life,
you find solace under the shadow of the sun's companion.
Seek God's friendship now,
for God will become your true friend.

38

Whoever deviates from their core
will once more seek their days of reunion.

39

To ensure that you are not left wanting
when you take your final breath,
carve and scratch down this path.

40

You have nothing but what you strive for;
the worth of effort lies in striving for what you want.
The Lord is the greatest giver of effort;
indeed, no one of low status is a part
of the kingdom of effort.

Part 5

Secrets to Beautiful Living

41

Giving up lust, greed, and wrath
is a sign of prophetic virtue and nobility.
Difficulties surround paradise,
while desires encircle hellfire.

42

Your bat's sense points westward,
while your jewel-foot's sense points eastward.
As the sense of the spirit feeds on sunlight,
the sense of the body thrives on darkness.

43

All people hold the view
that Almighty God controls everything,
and that not a single atom
in the heavens or on Earth is beyond His will.
I do not feel the need
to cry out, beg, or pray
for God's command to be changed,
because I am happy with it as it is,
regardless of what occurs.

44

Pleasant thoughts make patience easier
because they anticipate release.
Comfort originates from a person's deep faith;
a weak faith feeds grief and hopelessness.

45

Because it draws you nearer to the friend,
thankfulness is the essence of blessings,
while blessings are merely their outer layer.

46

Rich people and riches are rejected
because they lack patience due to their dominance.
Man's frailty and impoverishment
serve as a defense against tragedy and a hungry spirit.

47

Two yards' worth of scenery are visible to one eye,
and the king's face is visible to another.
The dervishes have transcended all of this,
and non-being is like being in the highest sky.
Stop complaining about your pain,
because it is he who is leading a horse
away from non-existence.

48

Trials become sweet when you perceive clarity,
and medicine becomes pleasurable
when health is restored.
When facing defeat,
you believe you have triumphed,
which is why you cry out,
'Kill me, O trusted ones!'

49

If you are watchful and awake,
you will see the response
to your actions in every moment.

50

Caution begets chaos;
trust is preferable.
Rely on trust.
O ferocious one,
do not wrestle with fate:
lest destiny wrestle with you in return.

Part 6

The Fate of the Materialist

51

The worldly are destitute and afraid;
they have no fear of those who would steal from them;
naked they came, and naked will they leave;
and the grief of thieves has wounded their hearts.

52

The one who was blinded by salt water
till he lost his sight
was the one who ignored the motions of the sea,
constantly turning to a different altar.

53

They find joy in degrading themselves
in the hopes of achieving honour,
enduring humiliation in the process.
They have lowered their heads,
sorrowful as a camel's load,
for the merest hope of glory.

54

'Your friends are but hunters,
seeking their prey at this hour,'
the blind man said.
Are you looking for blindness on the streets,
while your people are looking for graves
in the mountains?

55

You are indeed a slave to this time,
though you claim sovereignty over it.
The true master of this realm
is the one who strives against its destruction.
O you, captive of this world!
You have named yourself the ruler of this realm.

56

God gives dust and precious stones
amazing colours and qualities,
making little souls fight over them.
Children long for the bread
that they create from dough shaped
like camels and lions.
They will not believe you,
even if you tell them the truth.

57

There is no fruit in this world or its people;
they are both alike in their betrayal.
The child of the world is just as unfaithful as the rest.
Even if it were to reveal its face to you,
it would be cunning.

58

The titles of monarch, government, and lordship
keep death, suffering, and the loss
of life hidden from them.

59

Your life's cloth was ripped by the tailor of vanity,
and hacked to pieces by the scissors of time.

60

The efforts of the ignoble will eventually come to an end,
like the rotting of once-fresh fruit.
As the world is a place of creation and decay,
its affluence soon gives way to stagnation.

Part 7

The Characteristics of Followers of True Life

61

O you who are the mirror of royal beauty,
O you who are the heavenly script,
everything that is in the world is within you.
Look within for what you seek,
because you are everything.

62

Hope emerges from the depths of sorrow,
and a vision emerges from the heart
during the darkest moments.

63

Know that your lofty goals
are a mirror of your own will
if you have high expectations
for yourself, and high thinking.

64

Only take a seat next to someone who is heart-aware.
Walk beneath the flower-bearing tree.

65

Hold on to your secrets
and say not a word,
for if you remain silent,
what used to hurt will start to heal.

66

Sow only love and affection
in this pristine field,
in this soil.

67

Nothing, not even eating, sleeping, or walking,
can make friends feel better
when they are in the depths of sorrow –
only spending time with a friend can.

68

The elderly can see in a brick
what the young perceive in a mirror.

69

Betrayal goes against the creed of love;
I walk straight,
but it will not line up
if you walk unevenly.

70

Well-chosen words have the power to ignite an unlit lamp,
like a lit lamp kissing an extinguished one
with its own flame.

Part 8

The Role of Ethics
in Human Life

71

We look to God's grace to learn manners.
We lose the Lord's grace
when we lack manners.

72

The impolite person not only hurts themself,
but also enflames the whole planet.

73

All the gloom and sadness in your life
are the result of heedlessness and hubris.

74

See the shadow of Tuba[1] and get a good night's rest.
Sleep modestly and place your head in the shade.
You will soon become disobedient and lost
if you turn away from this shade in my direction.

---

1   A tree in Paradise.

75

Woe to presumption taken before monarchs;
O humility,
servant before the foolish.

76

Conceit stems from superficiality,
fed by riches and worldly standing.

77

One became so arrogant from that game
that they deviated from the teachers' precepts.

78

Because of the profound intoxication that existence brings, reason flees and guilt leaves the heart.

79

Choose this path and abandon self-centredness.
Give up 'me' and 'mine', and find peace;
this will make you delight in
the scent of flowers amongst lovers,
directing the garden in the manner of a guide.

80

Boiling water in oil will damage both the kettle
and the stove.
Talk gently, but never incorrectly.
Do not sell whispers in the marketplace of ideas.

Part 9

Essential Tools & Instruments of Life

81

Obtaining a living involves struggle and work;
each person is given a trade and a mission.
Seek food using their methods;
pass through their gates to reach other realms.

82

You would not make regrettable excuses
if you asked for guidance in that regard.
Because when two intelligent people are coupled,
it creates a barrier against bad words and deeds.

83

Give this to your ears and intelligence
as a reward for not attributing your own guilt
to someone else.
Accept justice and vengeance;
do not point the finger at others for your own mistakes,
as you yourself planted the seeds of them.

84

Instead of concentrating on your flaws,
focus on your ambitions.
Consider your high objectives
instead of thinking of yourself as weak, or 'lower'.

85

O soul,
give thought precedence over the Self,
for it is thinking that bestows value and vitality
upon the individual.

86

You have opened paths;
do not go where you should not.
Seek your own route;
do not become a hostage.

87

Friends suffer as much as the soul does,
and there are no indicators of friendship amongst friends.
When does a friend's suffering prevent them
from being friends anymore?
Friendship is the brain, and pain is its skin.

88

What is Justice?
What is in its proper place.
What is oppression?
What is not in its proper place.
What is Justice?
Irrigating the trees.
What is oppression?
Missing the thorns.

89

Nobody became a ruler,
no one lost their soul to greed,
and no one found contentment.

90

The intelligent man turns to face the impoverished,
who always adopts a middle position.
And moderation pays off.
When one element outweighs the others,
illness ensues.

Part 10

The Role of Good & Evil in Human Life

91

Poison in one location,
cure in another.
Belief in one area,
incredulity in another.
Even if juice from a pickle is sour,
it becomes sweet and delicious
when it comes from grape.

92

To enable the palm tree to grow tall and strong,
the gardener cuts off branches that pose a threat.
That weed is taken out of the garden
by the intelligent gardener,
making the garden and its produce appetizing to all.

93

When people of both sexes mingle,
beauty arises from the mixture of difference.

94

It separates each one from the other
if it blends its sugar and camphor.
The souls spread and the drums crack,
allowing good and evil to mix together.

95

From certain perspectives,
the world may appear pointless.
But from others,
it may, in fact, be advantageous.

96

There is no such thing
as absolute evil in the world;
evil is relative.

97

God grants the requests of the pious,
just as you wish.

98

Tools and methods are not inherited from the father;
all good and evil have a cause.
They are mere delusions on the main path,
passing through a period of ignorance.

99

Since God is supreme and has absolute power,
he can do as He pleases,
and heals suffering right from its source.

100

Men and women have grieved at my cries,
since they cut me from the reed bed.
To express the agony of longing,
I need a chest torn apart by separation.

Finis